THIS JOURNAL BELONGS TO:

____

Made in the USA
Monee, IL
13 January 2021

57466715R00069